Easiest Book Ever

How to spend less than $500 to have your book written for you

Contents

Chapter 1: Intro 4

Chapter 2: Write Outline 6

Chapter 3: Let our software write the book for you 22

Chapter 4: Design your book cover for free using Canva 24

Chapter 5: Edit your book 25

Chapter 6: Publish 27

Chapter 7: Closing 28

Chapter 8: Here is the outline we used for a demo book 29

Chapter 9: This is the unedited content that the software produced. 44

Chapter 1: Intro

Last year I got an email from a software developer. She told me that she had created a software that took the headache out of writing a book. I was interested, but skeptical. How could software possibly replace the art that is writing?

I decided to learn more, and watched a demo of the software. It took an outline, produced by the 'author' and it spit out a 10,000 word book. I was amazed.

The book needed a little editing- it was written by a computer after all, but after 2 hours of editing, it was ready to be published. This patent pending, proprietary software did what it was supposed to do!

It was at that point I was sold. I bought the software. And now have made it's use available to the public.

To demonstrate it's power, I've included an unedited version of what the software can do. Chapter 8 has the outline that I uploaded to the software, and Chapter 9 has the raw, unedited content that the software created. I wanted to show you how well it works, so you can make an educated decision to see if it's right for you.

This book also includes everything you need to know to get your book published- from start to finish. To see video demonstrations, head over to www.easiestbookever.com.

Chapter 2: Write Outline

The software uses a specific outline to create your book. Here is the template for that outline. I recommend writing the introductory chapter of the book yourself for 2 reasons. Reason number one is that it sounds like you and will keep people reading. Number 2 is that 57% of people never finish a book (even the really good ones). If the only information they get is the first chapter, you want to make sure that you summarize your most important points.

Book Title: **Easiest Book Ever**

Write your activity as a phrase beginning with a verb ending in -ING. (running a marathon)

```
┌─────────────────────────────────────┐
│                                     │
│                                     │
└─────────────────────────────────────┘
```

Transform this same activity into present tense (just take the -ING off of the verb). (run a marathon)

[   ]

Re-phrase your activity in a different way, still write it as a phrase beginning with a verb ending in -ING. (training for a marathon)

[   ]

Transform this same activity into present tense (just take the -ING off of the verb). (train for a marathon)

[   ]

Enter in an activity that opposes this activity (If "running a marathon" was my activity, I could put in "running the track in high school") Write your phrase beginning with a verb ending in -ING.

[   ]

Enter in a phrase of what someone who is successfully doing your activity is doing. Write your phrase beginning with a verb in present tense. f "running a marathon" was my activity, I could put in "winning a marathon"

[ ]

Write a word that is a noun that would describe someone who is successfully writing. In most instances, this would just be one single word. (someone who has run a marathon would be "champion")

[ ]

How long does your customer need to take to prepare to do the activity that you are going to show them how to do in this book?

[ ]

3 Questions your customer needs to ask themselves to see if it is a good fit for them (phrase the question so if they answer yes, it is a good fit for them). Next to this, enter a verb to describe this person. For example, 'Are you good a finding bargains?' this person would be a 'bargain hunter'

Question 1:

Verb:

Write one word that is an adjective that would describe someone who answered NO to your question. (Example: Do you refuse to give up? The person that answers "no" might be considered lazy)

Question 2:

Verb:

Write one word that is an adjective that would describe someone who answered NO to your question. (Example: Do you refuse to give up? The person that answers "no" might be considered lazy)

[   ]

Question 3:

[   ]

Verb:

[   ]

Write one word that is an adjective that would describe someone who answered NO to your question. (Example: Do you refuse to give up? The person that answers "no" might be considered lazy)

[   ]

Describe 3 Activities that someone who wants to do this thing would already be doing in daily life (use a verb ending in -ing)

Activity 1:

[   ]

Turn this activity to present tense

[   ]

Activity 2:

[   ]

Turn this activity to present tense

[   ]

Activity 3:

[   ]

Turn this activity to present tense

[   ]

Describe 3 activities that someone who wants to do this needs to do in order to prepare, three benefits they would receive from doing each activity, and rule they must follow while they are preparing to do this activity: (write the phrase beginning with -ing)

Activity 1:

[ ]

Transform this activity into present tense (remove -ing from the verb)

[ ]

Activity Benefit 1 (begin with a verb ending in -ing):

[ ]

Turn this benefit into present tense (take off -ing)

[ ]

Activity Benefit 2: (begin with a verb ending in -ing):

[ ]

Turn this benefit into present tense (take off -ing)

Activity Benefit 3: (begin with a verb ending in -ing):

Turn this benefit into present tense (take off -ing)

Rule:

Rule Benefit: (write the phrase starting with a verb in present tense)

Activity 2:

Transform this activity into present tense (remove -ing from the verb)

[   ]

Activity Benefit 1 (begin with a verb ending in -ing):

[   ]

Turn this benefit into present tense (take off -ing)

[   ]

Activity Benefit 2: (begin with a verb ending in -ing):

[   ]

Turn this benefit into present tense (take off -ing)

[   ]

Activity Benefit 3: (begin with a verb ending in -ing):

[ ]

Turn this benefit into present tense (take off -ing)

[ ]

Rule:

[ ]

Rule Benefit: (write the phrase starting with a verb in present tense)

[ ]

Activity 3

[ ]

Transform this activity into present tense (remove -ing from the verb)

[   ]

Activity Benefit 1 (begin with a verb ending in -ing):

[   ]

Turn this benefit into present tense (take off -ing)

[   ]

Activity Benefit 2: (begin with a verb ending in -ing):

[   ]

Turn this benefit into present tense (take off -ing)

[   ]

Activity Benefit 3: (begin with a verb ending in -ing):

[   ]

Turn this benefit into present tense (take off -ing)

[   ]

Rule:

[   ]

Rule Benefit: (write the phrase starting with a verb in present tense)

[   ]

Three tips that can help someone be more economical with this task/project.

[   ]

Advice on equipment related to your task/ project.

[   ]

Advice on preparing their mindset for your task/ project.

[   ]

Advice on a physical habit (wear comfortable shoes, take a multi vitamin, ect) that relates to your task/ project.

[   ]

Write 1 word that describes a person that would be doing this activity as a noun: (running a marathon would be a runner)

[   ]

Think of a famous person who is known for doing your task/project. What is a big milestone they met towards the beginning of their career.

[   ]

Describe 2 things that should NOT be doing BEFORE doing your task or project:

Describe two things that one should NOT do DURING your task/project (present tense)

Describe two things that one should NOT do AFTER doing your task/project (use past tense)

Describe two things that you should do after doing your task/project.

List three reasons why people would want to do your task/project (present tense)

3 Questions your customer needs to ask themselves to see if it is a good fit for them (phrase the question so if they answer yes, it is a good fit for them). Next to this, enter a verb to describe this person. For example, 'Are you good a finding bargains?' this person would be a 'bargain hunter'

Question 1:

| |
| |

Verb:

| |
| |

Question 2:

| |
| |

Verb:

| |
| |

Question 3:

Verb:

List three reasons why people would want to do your
task/project.

Chapter 3: Let our software write the book for you

Hopefully, you are as excited as I was by this software. The next step is to head over to www.easiestbookever.com/buy, enter payment, and send your outline to our team. We will put your outline in the software and we will return your manuscript within a week. It's that easy!

To get a better idea of how the software works- skip ahead to Chapters 8 and 9. Chapter 8 shows you the exact outline we used to create Chapter 9 with the software.

We have left the text in chapter 9 completely unedited so you can see the quality content the software produces.

Chapter 4: Design your book cover for free using Canva

Canva.com is my favorite graphic design software. It provides beautiful templates that let's you modify beautiful works of art and make your own.

To video an example of how to create your own book cover art visit www.easiestbookever.com/bookcover

Chapter 5: Edit your book

Pro tips for editing:

1. Let Word do some of the work. Spell/grammar check works well so use it!
2. Read the manuscript out loud. If it doesn't sound natural (it was written by a computer after all...) change it. It's much easier to catch mistakes by reading out loud.
3. Phone a friend. Ask someone not involved in the process to take a read through. They might catch things that you don't.

If editing really isn't your thing, go to Fiverr.com and pay someone to do it for you. I would verify that they are a native English speaker, and have some experience editing. Also, give the book a read through when you are done. You might catch something that they don't.

Once the content is edited, it needs to be formatted.

Head over to Createspace to get the latest updates on formatting.

Go to: Createspace -> Books -> Publish a trade paperback -> Interior -> Download the Createspace PDF Submission Specifications

Chapter 6: Publish

It's amazing how easy it is to self publish these days. Amazon bought Create Space- which makes the process nearly seamless.

Create Space provides a free ISBN number (the barcode number on the back of all books). This allows you to be able to sell at all major retailers. Make sure to select "expanded distribution" when you are publishing your book.

Chapter 7: Closing

In closing, this is the easiest way I know of to get a book written and published. Some gurus suggest creating books of quotes or a book of 10 tips and publishing that. I personally disagree with the philosophy. I think a 10,000 word book is the way to go if you are looking to establish yourself as an expert in your field. If you only have 6 pages of content to share with an audience, does it really show your expertise?

Whether you decide to use our software or not, I strongly encourage you to write a book. It can do loads for your credibility as an expert in your field.

Chapter 8: Here is the outline we used for a demo book

Book Title: **Easiest Book Ever**

Write your activity as a phrase beginning with a verb ending in -ING. (running a marathon)

writing

Transform this same activity into present tense (just take the -ING off of the verb). (run a marathon)

write

Re-phrase your activity in a different way, still write it as a phrase beginning with a verb ending in -ING. (training for a marathon)

publishing a book

Transform this same activity into present tense (just take the -ING off of the verb). (train for a marathon)

publish a book

Enter in an activity that opposes this activity (If "running a marathon" was my activity, I could put in "running the track in high school") Write your phrase beginning with a verb ending in -ING.

giving speeches

Enter in a phrase of what someone who is successfully doing your activity is doing. Write your phrase beginning with a verb in present tense. f "running a marathon" was my activity, I could put in "winning a marathon"

selling lots of books

Write a word that is a noun that would describe someone who is successfully writing. In most instances, this would just be one single word. (someone who has run a marathon would be "champion")

writer

How long does your customer need to take to prepare to do the activity that you are going to show them how to do in this book?

2 days

3 Questions your customer needs to ask themselves to see if it is a good fit for them (phrase the question so if they answer yes, it is a good fit for them). Next to this, enter a verb to describe this person. For example, 'Are you good a finding bargains?' this person would be a 'bargain hunter'

Question 1

Do you like to read books?

Verb:
reader

Write one word that is an adjective that would describe someone who answered NO to your question. (Example: Do you refuse to give up? The person that answers "no" might be considered lazy)

non-reader

Question 2

Do you have lots of content you want to share?

Verb:
content creator

Write one word that is an adjective that would describe someone who answered NO to your question. (Example: Do you refuse to give up? The person that answers "no" might be considered lazy)

boring

Question 3:

Do you need to establish yourself as an expert?

Verb:
expert

Write one word that is an adjective that would describe someone who answered NO to your question. (Example: Do you refuse to give up? The person that answers "no" might be considered lazy)

non-expert

Describe 3 Activities that someone who wants to do this thing would already be doing in daily life (use a verb ending in -ing)

2. presenting

Turn this activity to present tense

present

3. teaching

Turn this activity to present tense

teach

3   blogging

Turn this activity to present tense

blog

Describe 3 activities that someone who wants to do this needs to do in order to prepare, three benefits they would receive from doing each activity, and rule they must follow while they are preparing to do this activity: (write the phrase beginning with -ing)

Activity 1

Talking to people who would want to read your book

Transform this activity into present tense (remove -ing from the verb)

Talk to people who would want to read your book

Activity Benefit 1 (begin with a verb ending in -ing):

Understanding what they want to learn

Turn this benefit into present tense (take off -ing)

Understand what they want to learn

Activity Benefit 2: (begin with a verb ending in -ing):

Asking what questions they have

Turn this benefit into present tense (take off -ing)

Understand what they want to learn

Activity Benefit 3: (begin with a verb ending in -ing):

Making sure you are focused on the right topics

Turn this benefit into present tense (take off -ing)

Make sure you are focused on the right topics

Rule:

Listen intently to what they say

Rule Benefit: (write the phrase starting with a verb in present tense)

know the book will meet their needs

Activity 2 **Brainstorming your book idea**

Transform this activity into present tense (remove - ing from the verb)

Brainstorm your book idea

Activity Benefit 1 (begin with a verb ending in -ing):

Getting organized

Turn this benefit into present tense (take off -ing)

Get organized

Activity Benefit 2: (begin with a verb ending in -ing):

Making sure you are presenting your best content

Turn this benefit into present tense (take off -ing)

Make sure you are presenting your best content

Activity Benefit 3: (begin with a verb ending in -ing):

Showing the benefits of the book

Turn this benefit into present tense (take off -ing)

Show the benefits of the book

Rule:

Don't over think it

Rule Benefit: (write the phrase starting with a verb in present tense)

move forward confidently

Activity 3

Researching other books in the market

Transform this activity into present tense (remove -ing from the verb)

Research other books in the market

Activity Benefit 1 (begin with a verb ending in -ing):

getting topic ideas

Turn this benefit into present tense (take off -ing)

get topic ideas

Activity Benefit 2: (begin with a verb ending in -ing):

seeing what is selling well

Turn this benefit into present tense (take off -ing)

see what is selling well

Activity Benefit 3: (begin with a verb ending in -ing):

getting ideas for the book cover

Turn this benefit into present tense (take off -ing)

get ideas for the book cover

Rule:

don't get discouraged if there are a lot of books like yours

Rule Benefit: (write the phrase starting with a verb in present tense)

know there is always room for your unique content

Three tips that can help someone be more economical with this task/project.

1   design your own book cover using Canva

2   edit the book yourself

3   self publish on Createspace

Advice on equipment related to your task/ project.

Everything you need to get your book published is available to you for free. CreateSpace provides you with a free ISBN (the barcode on the back of all books). They also allow you to sell books through Barnes and Noble and other distributers at no additional cost. Make sure to select "expanded distribution" when you are publishing your book.

Advice on preparing their mindset for your task/ project.

Don't over think this- you don't have to create a masterpiece. In a lot of cases, done is good enough. 57% of books that are started are not read to completion.

Advice on a physical habit (wear comfortable shoes, take a multi vitamin, ect) that relates to your task/ project.

Wear comfortable clothes, and grab a cup of your favorite beverage. Wine helps me write better!

Write 1 word that describes a person that would be doing this activity as a noun: (running a marathon would be a runner)

writer

Think of a famous person who is known for doing your task/project. What is a big milestone they met towards the beginning of their career.

Getting your first book published is a huge milestone.

Describe 2 things that should NOT be doing BEFORE doing your task or project:

1   worry

2   stress

Describe two things that one should NOT do DURING your task/project (present tense)

1. Overthink your content

2. Procrastinating

Describe two things that one should NOT do AFTER doing your task/project (use past tense)

1. Don't get the book created, and not edit it. It does you no good in a drawer!

2. Don't neglect to let people know you wrote a book- shout it from the rooftops!

Describe two things that you should do after doing your task/project.

1. Tell people about it!

2. Carry a copy with you wherever you go

List three reasons why people would want to do your task/project (present tense)

1   establish yourself as an expert

2   get published

3   credibility

3 Questions your customer needs to ask themselves to see if it is a good fit for them (phrase the question so if they answer yes, it is a good fit for them). Next to this, enter a verb to describe this person. For example, 'Are you good a finding bargains?' this person would be a 'bargain hunter'

Question 1

Do you like to read books?

Verb:
         reader

Question 2

Do you have lots of content you want to share?

Verb:

content creator

Question 3

Do you need to establish yourself as an expert?

Verb:

expert

List three reasons why people would want to do your
task/project.

1	establish yourself as an expert

2	get published

3	credibility

Chapter 9: This is the unedited content that the software produced.

About Writing

Normally when a person reflects on writing, they contemplate giving speeches. The truth would be that the two may be polar opposites. If you are venturing to selling lots of books, there would be a few preparations you ought to make in order to reach your goals.

Here are some preparatory guidelines to get you off the ground:

-- Blogging

The key to thriving with writing would be

contingent on blogging, yet many individuals don't understand just how essential it really is! By blogging. you will make certain that you're equipped to write.

-- Presenting

Presenting helps you write. Understandably, it can be hard to get in the practice of doing it. Begin presenting every single day, and it will be habitual when you write.

-- Teaching

Teaching is so fundamental because without doing it, you will get non-expert. That will result in becoming incapable to write. There are definitely a handful of qualities that individuals ought to have in order to publish a book. So folks with these qualities will already teach regularly.

We wish to examine the journey to writing fruitfully. We will prepare you for a heightened aspect of victory. Please consider a couple things one ought to anticipate before looking to publish a book. Before writing, you must figure out and make sure that publishing a book is an appropriate choice for your lifestyle.

One of the best ways to decide whether you would be capable to write would be to look the regular practices of folks who already write regularly. You do not need to assimilate their accomplishments instantaneously, because that might be difficult. Though, you ought to be equipped to exert as much energy as they do. Mimic their practices, because they are specifically where you wish to be. In addition, contemplate the following questions:

Do you like to read books?

Do you have lots of content you want to share?

Do you need to establish yourself as an expert?

Ideally, your response to the questions was "yes". These habits are typical among those who write. You have now taken the first step towards writing!

Since you understand that you need to be in the proper mindset to write, we will examine a handful of preliminary practices that an individual writing will already be carrying out. Use this opportunity to absorb these specific practices into your activities because it will make preparing to write easier.

Writing entails loads of energy invested over time. So you will see, the best way to get equipped for writing would be to allow yourself the suggested amount of time for the training so you can be successful. Do this, and writing would be much easier.

Writing - A Look Back

In the event you have been thinking about writing, be informed you will have a tough road ahead. If it was easy, anybody would achieve it. A lot of individuals who decide to publish a book end up not actually following through.

Writing needs your mental energy equally as much as it needs your physical energy. Clearly, writing would be really physical, however through having a very strong mind you could train yourself for victory.

Despite how far back you might care to look, you will find that those who are writing have one big thing in common: they understood what they were getting into. They understood what it was going to be similar to, everything that writing involved, and everything that was required of them to successfully accomplish their main objective. When you understand what it entails to write, there would be nothing to stop you!

Don't reflect on giving speeches. Writing requires an individual to be reader and determined. We recognize that. Now we are ready to investigate the steps recommended with writing so we could enjoy our forthcoming success.

You had previously asked yourself: "Do you like to read books?" Reasonably, you had to ask this to yourself. Anyone that answered no to this will remain powerless to take any action to write.

You have previously also considered whether you are content creator as soon as you were asked: Do you have lots of content you want to share? Pat yourself on the back on making it this far, because it means you clearly have not surrendered. There is a big difference between doing one thing and wanting to do something. That will come up quite a bit in publishing a book.

You've already begun a huge step towards becoming equipped to write. A lot of individuals fail for a logical reason. They frankly did not understand the things that they are getting themselves into. Writing is that one thing in life that requires you to get entirely steadfast and prepared. By looking at what's before you and making sure you are reader and content creator, you are taking the first step toward preparing.

Just know, blogging is essential. Every time your mind relays that writing is unattainable, just recognize that an individual who is blogging will move past the negativity and keep their attention toward success. Let's examine what is essential to prevail since our thoughts are where we need it to be!

Writing In Everyday Life

Writing may not be an action which you decide to do daily, however if you look at the effects of writing, you may incorporate that in your regular life. The truth is that writing includes side effects which will benefit other parts of life.

You may remember when we analyzed a handful of questions. We were in order to determine if writing was an action that is sensible for you to do. These following questions are really lifestyle questions:

Do you like to read books?

Do you have lots of content you want to share?

Do you need to establish yourself as an expert?

Along with evaluating your lifestyle, these questions are also looking to analyze your capabilities and desires. So if you replied yes to these questions, there would be an implication of everything that is significant to you.

By recognizing the role these qualities play in your day-to-day life, you are understanding the role that writing plays in life. Writing is not easy. Many rewarding activities need commitment. Writing is no different.

Writing is more than giving speeches. It is a lifestyle option in numerous ways. When you evaluate it it way, you will realize the many benefits in general life. Fundamentally, it takes a special attribute to accomplish the final goal. It is beneficial to allow these benefits to alter your lifestyle all around.

Every time you publish a book, you would be spending a great deal of time. Ultimately, you are competing against yourself. The content creator quality which is essential to publish a book, alternatively, enhances your overall life. When you write you physically rely on yourself for energy. That would be specifically what makes writing possible.

While you're talk ingto people who would want to read your book, brainstorming your book idea or researching other books in the market, you may just be trying to achieve general betterment. With honing in on the lifestyle, something will become abundantly clear and you may see everything that writing actually means to you. If you would realize the effects of writing, you may come to understand that those effects are really what you are trying to experience.

The best thing about writing would be the reader quality that would be needed to succeed which will make its way in all parts of life. That causes you to be a more reader person overall. Every time you publish a book, you are preparing yourself for that which may follow. It would be just one of the good things of writing.

The most devoted individuals will see their main objective through. You might be one of these individuals. If you would allow your mind to be expert, you'd find the journey is an a thrilling one and kudos for taking that first step!

Why Write

Writing has become an increasingly sought-after activity among individuals everywhere. There are endless intentions to write, which is the reason many individuals try to do it. Writing may be done to establish yourself as an expert, to get published, or to credibility. Even though the probable intentions for writing are endless, there would be a few that stick out as the most common.

Establish Yourself As An Expert

Writing to establish yourself as an expert would be a great rationale to publish a book. Every time you have a clear-cut rationale to write, it makes the ambition more critical. Then when you ultimately selling lots of books, it should feel sweeter.

Get Published

A normal reason that many individuals elect to write would be to get published. That would be an excellent rationale to write as well.

Credibility

A different rationale which people choose to write would be to credibility. Publishing a book is a tough feat. Once you write successfully, you will also develop a unique bond with others that have also write.

Overall, writing will bring a huge feeling of success to your lifestyle, and for good reason. Briefing for this would be a thrilling experience, which is the one reason that many individuals decide to publish a book. In addition, writing could also allow you a new perspective on life. And as soon as you write, you should realize that you can accomplish just about anything else in life. That would be, if you would clear your mind and do it. The intentions to write are absolutely different from one person to the next. Thus ultimately, you ought to do it for your own personal reasons.

Things To Do Before Writing

A guide full of stuff to accomplish before writing will surely fill up many full-length books. Writing is hard. It is clearly reflected through the massive amount of instructional material accessible to folks trying to publish a book. Despite this fact, there are a few effective ideas which every writer could make to their regimented schedule. It also, doesn't matter how qualified that writer is; you could make it work. The most essential requirement to keep in mind is that you'd have to prevail, both physically and mentally.

Talk ingto people who would want to read your book would be the key of every routine. You will never be capable to write if you only work on preparing a little bit every now and then. Complete a regimented schedule and stick with it. It would be okay to take some days off every now and then, but you ought to be relatively steadfast with preparing each day. Talk ingto people who would want to read your book daily will encourage you in a multitude of ways. You will even start to feel differently.

You will be better equipped for any obstacle because you would get stronger. You will definitely think better about yourself overall. Remember that you're a reader person, and you ought to make all necessary changes to reflect that. Get in the practice of talk ingto people who would want to read your book so you are constantly understanding what they want to learn and asking what questions they have.

Equally essential as talk ingto people who would want to read your book would be brainstorming your book idea. When you observe individuals who have efficiently write, you will see that they constantly brainstorm your book idea. It is because they understand the importance of this practice. Brainstorming your book idea results in getting organized. It is commonly known that brainstorming your book idea also will make sure you are presenting your best content. Don't over think it. It will move forward confiedently.

Crowds of people will agree that they would be showing the benefits of the book, solely by brainstorming your book idea. That will get your brain on structuring your regular responsibilities to write. When publishing a book, it should encourage you to bear in mind the reason you are doing it in the first place. You will also remember which preparatory guidelines and techniques have worked for you before.

Another great benefit that a writer has is when they research other books in the market. They would be getting topic ideas. Being ready to write swiftly is important. But it will be futile if you are incapable of writing for a long time. Researching other books in the market has a multitude of positive effects which go beyond publishing a book. Researching other books in the market results in getting topic ideas and seeing what is selling well.

There are a few other considerations to bear in mind when you're researching other books in the market. Don't get discouraged if there are a lot of books like yours. It will directly churn out a better result to know there is always room for your unique content. Furthermore, researching other books in the market will encourage you to get ideas for the book cover. And through having a really optimistic point-of-view, it will assist you with any discouraging hours you might have. Think about what you could try to enhance your activities, and proceed from there. An optimistic point-of-view will make a big difference when you're writing.

Classic Mistakes Made While You Write

Undoubtedly, there may be a few steps that you'll not want to do while publishing a book. Even though every new writer will make a handful of errors, there are two in particular that you'd want to prevent at all costs.

Do not don't get the book created, and not edit it. it does you no good in a drawer!. It will cause you to fall back in your efforts. Why would anyone put in all that effort only to reverse what they have done? That is what takes place when you don't get the book created, and not edit it. it does you no good in a drawer!.

There's something that will help you prevent certain blunders from developing. If you have been publishing a book for a while, designate some time off to divide up all training involved.

In addition, don't stress. It would be the other essential blunder that any writer could avoid. Even though there are many ideas to publish a book, following these recommendations will churn out a really positive result no matter what. Provided you're consistent with your responsibilities and follow through the preparations, then you will be capable to selling lots of books.

Rules to Consider While Writing

Briefing to write requires an individual to be reader, content creator and expert. At times these qualities can be brought out of an individual when specific tips are followed. This section will examine those tips that have been purposefully designed to cultivate those particular qualities.

Briefing for writing takes some footwork. Most of these guidelines will be ingrained in your head during this process. Since you will possibly be spending around 2 days on preparing, you should have enough time to really focus on these rules.

Just Listen intently to what they say. This is particularly pertinent when you're talk ingto people who would want to read your book, because it will know the book will meet their needs. It isn't the only great benefit that following this rule will bring. Also asking what questions they have and making sure you are focused on the right topics would be other benefits which also produce the most noticeable results.

Also, remember that those who productively brainstorm your book idea will always Don't over think it. It is incredible how these simple guidelines could be such a vital factor in a bigger goal. When you see yourself as see who is content creator, then you may find it relatively simple to include these tips into your regimented process. Furthermore, if you choose to Don't over think it, then it will move forward confiedently.

You ought to consistently have your focus concentrated on researching other books in the market. That might compel you to be even more focused when you train, and this is certainly worth it. It also helps you get topic ideas. Just Don't get discouraged if there are a lot of books like yours.

This will know there is always room for your unique content, which will proceed to see what is selling well.

Truthfully, it takes a expert person to reach the end goal of writing. It is not impossible to publish a book regardless, but really you would still have to be reader. Keep in mind, we are absolutely not preparing for giving speeches. Writing not only requires a state of mind that is content creator, but more importantly one which is fully committed to the goal.

When making a commitment to thoroughly prepare, it would be your job to not drop out! Do you remember when you answered these few questions:

Do you like to read books?

Do you have lots of content you want to share?

Do you need to establish yourself as an expert?

To all of the three questions, you replied yes. This is great because we wanted to determine whether you were content creator, reader and expert. It is these great qualities that will lead you towards your victory when you ultimately write. Thus, remember to talk to people who would want to read your book, brainstorm your book idea, and research other books in the market. Follow these specific instructions and you will be a writer in no time!

What You Need to Know Before Writing

We examined a couple of the various practices that anyone who expects to write could contemplate carrying out. Since you have recognized the habits of an individual wanting to write, odds are that a few habits are spliced into your regular activities already. You could examine how you could propogate these tendencies into a greater part of your routine. That will make preparing to write a painless evolution.

Nevertheless, preparing to accomplish the final goal will compel you to adhere to a couple changes in your activities. Your receptiveness to growing will be the determining factor in how swiftly you realize your calling.

Are you equipped to present? Are you equipped to teach and blog? These are only a handful of practices to strengthen you with the journey of writing. If it seems staggering, don't agonize. We have a couple recommendations pertaining to achieving your ambitions.

Don't rush through the preparatory stages.

Sometimes it seems as though the preparatory stages may be disregarded. Concievably you may think you may overcome without carrying out measures like presenting. There will probably come a time after beginning the preparation of writing where you will face a task such as talk ingto people who would want to read your book. If you performed the preparatory stages noted, you will face an increasingly smoother time achieving your ambitions.

Investing a fixed amount of time solely to focus on the subsidiary measures would be best. It will cause the following part of your journey to be smoother. Ultimately, you will be fully equipped to write after the preparation.

Don't give up if you fail preparing.

Regardless how critical your effort may be, expect problems. Instead of attempting perfection, consider following the preparatory stages for the majority of the day. That will allow you a cushion to botch up the preparations periodically. If you count on faltering from perfection periodically, it will prevent you from surrendering in the time you stumble from the preparations of writing.

Everything you need to get your book published is available to you for free. CreateSpace provides you with a free ISBN (the barcode on the back of all books). They also allow you to sell books through Barnes and Noble and other distributers at no additional cost. Make sure to select "expanded distribution" when you are publishing your book.

It might appear like an indisputable thing to accomplish when you are preparing to write. Though it is surprising how some individuals fail getting appropriate supplies beforehand. It would be a painless tip to consider. Don't make the most critical misstep of rushing through these fundamental preparations.

Don't over think this- you don't have to create a masterpiece. In a lot of cases, done is good enough. 57% of books that are started are not read to completion.

Whether you're venturing to successfully accomplish a tangible ambition or an integral part of the process which entails more mental energy, your brain leads what you do. That would be the reason, it would be essential to train yourself with the production at hand. When the mind is geared for the production at hand, it results in carrying out the work quicker. Whatever we achieve begins with a hope. Plant positive ideas in your brain, and the journey to write will be totally underway.

When you contemplate surrendering, don't.

It would be normal to get discouraged when things become hard. If writing was simple, anybody would be doing it. The truth would be that writing entails some energy and calculated action. The benefits would be really fulfilling. Even though you may want to give up when things become hard, don't. Don't give up because you could achieve this!

Ignore all perceptions you have concerning writing.

With television, the Net and social media so rampant in our routine, it would be possible to have preconceived thoughts about writing. Most of the perceptions concerning writing are not exactly accurate. Assume hard effort and devotion to achieve the ambitions of writing. Regardless how you evaluate it, a reader and content creator individual will thrive at writing. If you are incapable to identify yourself as content creator and reader currently, don't agonize. These qualities are cultivated and you must nurture yourself to become reader and content creator.

Wear comfortable clothes, and grab a cup of your favorite beverage. Wine helps me write better!

Even though writing begins with a journey with yourself, there would be the tangible aspect which would be equally integral. While the will is in a proper place, you really have to work all tangible preparations. These recommendations are so essential because it focuses on the tangible aspect of writing.

These are several distinct practices which will

prepare you for the experience. You ought to plan to spend about 2 days to publish a book. Prior to when the 2 days starts, you ought to be following these specific suggestions. A commitment entails a moment to bring into action. It begins with a pledge in the mind. Keep a journal to record the growth and it will encourage you to remain on track.

If you go off track, get immediately back on. Writing is a journey and periodically you may go off track. The essential thing would be that you get immediately back on! Also, make sure that you're reveling in your experience. Anyone that yearns to write expects to receive some mental gratification from it. Also feed off the recognition you receive along the way when you eventually selling lots of books!

The Easiest Way To Write

Even though there are plenty of books available about writing, there's one particular message they all reveal: the planning phase is very essential. A decent period of time to publish a book would be on average 2 days. Briefing for this long offers you the essential energy to write.

You are now totally ready to get into the task at hand. But, first we'll go over a few positive practices. That way you're as equipped as possible once you write. The following steps that you could do to get ready to write are: present, teach and blog. All together these tips form a strong core for your training.

Then for the 2 days that you designate to prepare for writing, focus on talk ingto people who would want to read your book, brainstorming your book idea and researching other books in the market. The biggest blunder that some individuals make while trying to write is neglecting planning. Now that you are informed, be sure to designate 2 days of planning before writing.

When you disregard these specific guidelines, you will forego understanding what they want to learn, asking what questions they have, and making sure you are focused on the right topics. These results all stem from the planning phase.

If you would invest in publishing a book, then you may find that it is shockingly easier than you may anticipate. The right planning primes you to be totally ready. That results in making sure you are focused on the right topics, showing the benefits of the book and getting ideas for the book cover. These benefits better position you to effectively write. That being said, don't solely dart through the preparations because all these benefits are equally essential.

Sometimes, when observing people who effectively write, it could be easy to think that they have magical energy or know some secret trick which permits them to be a writer. However, there's no secret. Writing only takes an individual who is reader, content creator and expert. By making the time to make certain that your efforts are really working, you would be capable to write at a fast pace.

It may appear like a quite a long time to put in, but really 2 days generally tends to fly by. It would be normal to think this way, particularly while preparing for something as huge as writing. Provided you continue to put in the proper effort, you will be writing in no time. Writing will be hard. However, through preparing the most effective way, you will be sure to overcome it!

Writing For Free

You may think that it costs a great deal of cash to write, but in fact you could publish a book for free. The main thing you could do when you start to publish a book would be to remove all existing beliefs you may possibly have concerning what it would be like.

There are only three rudimentary instructions which will help you even out your dreams of writing with your bank account. Design your own book cover using Canva. When you can focus on luxuries that don't need a lot of money, then you let yourself to focus on what exactly you ought to be carrying out. Keep in mind, talk ingto people who would want to read your book, brainstorming your book idea and researching other books in the market are areas that are of utmost importance and do not need loads of cash.

Expending additional money would not likely make you write any better. Thus, don't go looking for stores to blow your paycheck when you publish a book. Edit the book yourself. There are always free or affordable alternatives that successfully accomplish what you would be trying to do.

When you're researching other books in the market, accomplish it with a mindset to save cash. Self publish on Createspace. When you're writing you don't have to blow cash on overly high-priced options when there are inexpensive alternatives which work equally as great. Most individuals had been writing before many of the more high-priced options were created. If they didn't need it, then you will not either.

The best advice is certainly to hold your main objective as the main priority. More specifically, talk ingto people who would want to read your book, brainstorming your book idea and researching other books in the market are areas you should probably focus your focus. When you really analyze your emotions, it is much simpler to recognize when you're throwing away cash on stuff you do not need.

Talk ingto people who would want to read your book doesn't need a lot of cash. The aspiration would be to understand what they want to learn, and it could be realized with low spending because it doesn't have to be cost prohibitive. In actuality, it typically costs even more to not brainstorm your book idea. The reason you ought to focus on brainstorming your book idea would be so you can get organized. Again, it doesn't need a lot of spending to achieve.

Researching other books in the market would be another thing that your mind ought to be focused on because it is extremely essential for a person who expects to write. Even though there might be high-priced alternatives that appear great, you could naturally research other books in the market without being required to pay for it.

The final summation is, if you'd be steadfast on your objectives, then you could eliminate wasteful spending to achieve your objective of writing. There are always alternatives available that are minimal in cost. Understanding how your emotions influence your spending will better position you to maintain expenses when you're working towards writing.

Writing - Step by Step

From this point, it is understood what specific kind of person it takes to effectively write. We have also learned more about the qualities that an individual requires in order to publish a book. So now, we will now get serious with what exactly we are set to achieve.

It's essential that you be mindful that talk ingto people who would want to read your book is the most essential part in publishing a book. Talk ingto people who would want to read your book would be the most fundamental part in any preliminary routine. Without this, there are no way whatsoever that you would be ready to tackle writing. The best way to fruitfully succeed at writing would be talk ingto people who would want to read your book while you prepare.

Talk ingto people who would want to read your book has many great benefits. For one, it constantly results in you understanding what they want to learn. Without this, it will be tough to write. Another great benefit of talk ingto people who would want to read your book is it will have you asking what questions they have while making sure you are focused on the right topics.

So you also have to keep brainstorming your book idea throughout your preparations, and when you write. To publish a book is incredibly hard, but brainstorming your book idea will help. Plus, talk ingto people who would want to read your book will help you start getting organized, which is clearly important. Getting organized will help you when you publish a book now and in the days ahead.

The other benefits of brainstorming your book idea, as it pertains to writing, include making sure you are presenting your best content and showing the benefits of the book. In actuality, if you're not taking some specific kind of action into showing the benefits of the book, then it may be difficult to successfully accomplish anything considerable. Thus, if you elect against writing, then you still should probably consider activities that result in showing the benefits of the book.

After spending time toward talk ingto people who would want to read your book and brainstorming your book idea, you probably think you're equipped to write. Despite your perceptions, be sure to analyze whether you actually are or if it is only your mind leading you to think you are. A lot of individuals who are looking to write spend up to 2 days preparing.

Another requirement that would be needed to help you be successful with writing is researching other books in the market. You do not have to focus on researching other books in the market until the second half of the preparations, though certainly don't move past it altogether. Researching other books in the market could guide you to get topic ideas, and would be beneficial for the preparations. It also pushes you to see what is selling well and get ideas for the book cover, which in turn pushes you to write.

Ultimately, you'd be equipped to write through talk ingto people who would want to read your book, brainstorming your book idea and researching other books in the market. It generally takes 2 days of the preparation period to get totally prepared. But, that period of time will dart by extremely swiftly. If you would schedule a specific date to initiate your preparations and mark 2 days later, then it will better position your brain to see that timeframe as the preparation process. From that point, you'll be ready to focus on talk ingto people who would want to read your book, and brainstorming your book idea. Then, you'll find that your entire mind is totally prepared to write!

Strategies To Writing

Writing entails a lot from any person. Unfortunately, every person doesn't even have everything that it takes. There are definitely some clear-cut strategies that work more efficiently than others to assure that you're consistently preparing for your ambitions the right way. Acknowledging this will better position you to eventually write.

Publishing a book requires an individual to become devoted. Thus, an individual that is non-reader, or boring, may not likely be as fruitful as they could be. These qualities are within an individual who might have said no when approached with the question:

Do you like to read books?

There are qualities for which anyone wanting to write ought to have, and becoming reader is certainly one of them. The notion behind it is straightforward. Having a reader spirit is specifically what allows you to claim yourself as a writer after you productively write.

Anyone can declare that they wish to write. However, writing would be a huge step above giving speeches. One doesn't require a great deal of planning, whereas planning is certainly essential to the overall outcome of the other.

Presenting is a vital tactic in getting ready to write. However, folks usually misconstrue the importance of this. The truth remains that presenting is required for publishing a book. On a different note, writing alternatively helps additional parts in our regular lives.

Teaching might be a no-brainer just because it would be important for overall success when you write. Teaching would be essential while you publish a book simply considering what's all needed.

Blogging may also not seem like a huge thing, however it unquestionably is. When writing, you would need the training which you invested time on.

The strategies to writing assist not just the ambition of publishing a book, but each step really includes a variety of great benefits which will complement other parts in your lifestyle. It's straightforward to determine that understanding what they want to learn isn't only a great benefit to writing, but for life overall. Correspondingly, getting organized is known to assist other areas of life. Even getting topic ideas will be beneficial outside of writing. Other than becoming a writer, some people will enjoy how writing improves their lifestyle overall.

You may find when you use these great strategies to write that all present qualities you had will be significantly enhanced. Those who are definitely reader become much more reader. Correspondingly, folks who are content creator feel much more content creator. These are among the multiple specific reasons to start writing now!

Tips To Write Better

Writing would be a life-changing responsibility, but there are methods to make your lifestyle a bit more easier when you're publishing a book. Below are a few ideas for writing which will help you.

- Talk ingto people who would want to read your book has already been examined in great detail, and this would be rather essential when you're writing. Make sure that you know the book will meet their needs. Also, make it a practice to Listen intently to what they say. That doesn't only concern writing, it actually pertains to your lifestyle in general.

- You should understand that brainstorming your book idea would be important as well. It may seem hard to make happen on your own. Thus a great way to move forward confiedently would be to Don't over think it. This will allow you more reasons to brainstorm your book idea as you make preparations to write.

- Also, understand that writing requires you to constantly research other books in the market. In order to know there is always room for your unique content, it is beneficial to Don't get discouraged if there are a lot of books like yours.

Writing will lead you to acquire a lot of benefits, particularly as more time goes by. When you write, you may have the following benefits:

- When you talk to people who would want to read your book, you will start understanding what they want to learn.

- Talk ingto people who would want to read your book alternatively allows your body to start asking what questions they have more often.

- Brainstorming your book idea will result in getting organized.

- Furthermore, brainstorming your book idea helps with making sure you are presenting your best content.

- As you work to research other books in the market, you should find that you are seeing what is selling well.

- Researching other books in the market equally results in getting ideas for the book cover.

There would be some common benefits which take place when publishing a book. Making sure you are focused on the right topics and showing the benefits of the book are both distinct benefits of talk ingto people who would want to read your book and brainstorming your book idea. These benefits will contribute to lifestyle beyond writing. Similarly, researching other books in the market contributes to getting topic ideas. To reap those other benefits, following are a couple more instructions which will help you successfully accomplish your objective of publishing a book.

- Design your own book cover using Canva.

- Edit the book yourself.

- Self publish on Createspace.

Writing takes a great deal of energy. Thankfully, if you apply the guidance offered here when you publish a book, then you will be more than capable by the end of the 2 days to write.

The instructions which are noted here serve a

beginning point. Once going over this information, you'll have an appreciation of everything that it entails to write. Take the initiative to add your personal notes and develop new recommendations to encourage you be successful.

The Best System For Writing

There may be heaps of systems accessible to folks thinking more on writing, and they all claim to be the most simple. In fact, a couple of these specific systems, which you may uncover online, assure better benefits. Though, the accomplishment of writing depends on each person and their point-of-view towards planning. A great writer will be a great writer regardless what the situation. Correspondingly, a bad writer will continue to get worse regardless if they are writing for the first time, or are more qualified in their craft. Writing would be a mental activity equally as much as it would be a physical one.

Over the 2 days of preparing leading up to the big moment, you might get relatively busy planning in advance. Not only does publishing a book physically challenge you, but it equally stimulates your mind. In regards to planning the whole method, multi-faceted training is certainly essential. There may be heaps of tools handy to help determine the particulars of writing. However, your personal judgment must be a better alternative versus any tool. After all, you understand your body and state of mind like no one else. Apply that information to calculate your goal and don't ignore your intuition because it is not likely to misguide you.

We calculated that the normal amount of time an individual trains to write is 2 days. Thus, you ought to be generous while planning your time. Keep in mind, you understand your body much better than anyone. In the event you need more time, don't strain yourself trying to attain your ambition in specifically 2 days. Do the calculations and then measure the time you'd need. Lastly, adjust your objectives accordingly.

When you make preparations to write, you may uncover other people that may be trying to successfully accomplish the precise goal. Keep in mind, they're possibly working with a different timeframe than you. Thus, don't become caught up competing with their timetable or techniques if it doesn't work with your everyday rhythm. That is specifically how some people become burned out and ultimately bail out. You have previously begun the initial big step. Thus, work at your own pace. Another bad idea would be to make hasty decisions to adjust the timeframes inappropriately. Start out slow and then gradually invest more energy toward your plan as the preparations progress. That guarantees you'll be totally equipped to write.

Even though these strategies detailed here aren't foolproof, they're the best starting points for newbies trying to write. There are absolutely a lot of recommendations that you could include to fit your preparatory process, since you know your state of mind. Apply the information, and the plan produced here to jump out there and ultimately write! If you're consistent with how you spend your time, and fully use the information here to calculate a workable method, then you'll be a great writer in no time!

Do's and Don'ts of Writing

The thought of writing may be exhilarating and frightening. The distinguished Getting your first book published is a huge milestone would be a huge enhancement in any writer's career. Initially it might appear unattainable. Though, with the proper priming and foresight, writing could be mastered by anybody. Just as any trying challenge, writing may be mastered in a multitude of ways. Following are a couple things which every writer ought to (and ought to not) anticipate:

Before Writing

Even though the challenge is writing, there would be various considerations which every writer could achieve beforehand. That will assure that writing is not an insurmountable challenge.

DO Present

If you wish to write, you ought to be spending ample time preparing. That will physically encourage you to get topic ideas and see what is selling well.

DON'T Don't Get The Book Created, And Not Edit It. It Does You No Good In A Drawer!

It can be easy to neglect granting yourself time off from preparing. However, the day of recreation primes the mind to contemplate the ambition of writing. Grant yourself time to contemplate achieving your ambitions so you avoid fatigue.

DO Teach

The preparatory stages to writing is essential and by incorporating this simple tip of teaching, you will be carrying out what you could to prepare.

DON'T Stress

If you oversee every milestones at the heart of the training, it should not negatively impact the whole plan assuming you invest the energy to get back on track. Avoid the inclination to boosts the training disproportionately, because doing so may push you to lose momentum.

While Writing

DO Talk To People Who Would Want To Read Your Book

Recognize what you could achieve. Set your ambitions respectively. By incorporating this tip, you will understand what they want to learn and ask what questions they have. In addition, you will also make sure you are focused on the right topics.

DON'T Don't Get The Book Created, And Not Edit It. It Does You No Good In A Drawer!

The most qualified writer would be able to write quicker. That would be because they may have personal experience. Save your energy and avoid examining yourself with another writer and compare your growth only with yourself.

DO Brainstorm Your Book Idea

This would be an important tip. By following this tip in your career, you will understand what they want to learn and ask what questions they have. Also, you will make sure you are focused on the right topics.

DON'T Procrastinate

There would be no rationale to analyze theories pertaining to writing. Following are clear-cut criteria of what you should and should not achieve in order to thrive and eventually selling lots of books.

After Writing

After preparing to write, remember, the journey is not done! Here are a few do's, and don'ts, to recognize as soon as you achieve the goal:

DO Tell People About It!

DON'T Don't Get The Book Created, And Not Edit It. It Does You No Good In A Drawer!

DO Carry A Copy With You Wherever You Go

DON'T Don't Neglect To Let People Know You Wrote A Book- Shout It From The Rooftops!

These are a handful of fairly simple preparatory guidelines to reflect while writing. Recognize the journey and remember that the journey is yours!

How Writing Will Change You

Writing is not for the weak-hearted. It can get incredibly hard and the project does not become easier. Though, if you will brave the project to the finish line, you may find you aren't the same type of person that you were before you started. Despite how effectively you train, something about even trying to write provides so many additional benefits.

For starters, you realize how to write. Whether you overcome or fail, understanding how to prepare would be valuable to know. Despite all wealth of guidance and knowledge which you can find online or in self-help books, trying to write provides unique insights into how the numerous strategies work. That specific kind of insight not only results in understanding yourself better, but more importantly gives you much required information for future endeavors.

Fundamentally, writing proves how fully committed you are. Writing would be a goal that many people have, but barely a few have the dedication and focus to compete. Writing proves your devotion through the eyes of different people, but more importantly it verifies it to you. The guts and the willpower it entails to finish publishing a book should not go away as soon as you successfully accomplish your feat. Rather, they will remain a part of you.

Writing helps your mind through showing you have what it takes to selling lots of books. Writing also boosts brainpower. Once you write, you might be astonished by how you have made it to this point both intellectually and physically. You will be feeling these beneficial effects for many years.

Ultimately, writing offers you bragging rights. So now, not only could you share the exhilarating details of writing, with your friends, but you could share the stages of preparation. More importantly, you realize what you may be capable of. Writing entails loads of courage, and knowing you have what it takes to do something so tough.

Writing definitely would be difficult and challenging, but it changes you in many ways. It would be no wonder that only a handful of people thrive with writing. You would be showing yourself and the universe that you have the capabilities and insight to do some greater things in life!

Writing - The Lifestyle

It is instantly clear that individuals who strive to write come in all shapes and sizes. Though no matter the skill level, there are a handful of considerations which are normal among the individuals that wish to write. The reason loads of individuals who write have that vibe would be because every one of them have a lifestyle with corresponding values. This does not mean such people live parallel lives, because that would be ridiculous, and wrong. Those who write come from all walks of life. Even though such people may not all have everything in common, there may be a handful of lifestyle traits and tendencies that they all have.

Obviously the routine involves presenting. Without it, writing will feel difficult. Though, presenting is not strictly specific to only writing. Also, the routine involves teaching and blogging. Publishing a book will need talk ingto people who would want to read your book and brainstorming your book idea. The truth is that publishing a book would be an investment. Also, researching other books in the market can lead to many types of unexpected benefits.

Because of this, many individuals who want to write, especially those that are determined, will immediately recognize these additional benefits. These benefits do not develop exclusively from talk ingto people who would want to read your book, either. After spending so much energy in preparing your everyday life to write, all individuals will find themselves naturally making better everyday choices within other aspects of life. Those who have write may find that they would be ready to understand what they want to learn and ask what questions they have. Even though it isn't a magical skill that you will gain when you decide to write, it would be one thing which will gradually incorporate itself in your routine the further you prepare to publish a book.

These benefits are greater, but it could get really easy to get swept away without even seeing it. If you have many friends that also are looking to write, you might find that a few of them rarely focus energy on anything else but writing. As with any routine choice, a little careful moderation would be required.

As you train for writing, you should find that these specific lifestyle changes are developing in your activities. Talk ingto people who would want to read your book and brainstorming your book idea is beneficial in many ways, and thus, you would understand what they want to learn and get organized. The lifestyle would be very hard, but it would be definitely worth it. If you tough it out, writing and the associated routine will make your lifestyle better in numerous ways.

Is Writing Right For You?

Those who decide to write are extremely determined. There are many aspects in life which can't be faked. You can't fake a job interview, or the results of finals in college. Correspondingly, you can't fake writing. You frankly can't write without a little foresight. Publishing a book entails an individual to get reader and determined. It entails 2 days of preparing vigilantly.

While you are preparing your routine to write, be sure that you don't don't get the book created, and not edit it. it does you no good in a drawer!. In addition, don't look to stress. Preparation entails time and it must not be rushed. By rushing through the preparatory process, you would not truly be preparing and it could be concluded that you faked your way through the preparations. Doing it the proper way would allow you to have longevity toward your results.

Writing could get quite exhilarating and offers a feeling of success that you will value for life. Writing would be a challenge. Whether you would be just starting or are totally qualified, there are rational pros and cons of writing.

There are more benefits of writing and the main one would be that it will allow you a feeling of pride and success. Publishing a book is a tough activity. Writing would be something that might constantly remind you of your devotion and allow you a feeling of gratification for even trying this activity.

A different great benefit of writing would be that it perfects your preparation skills because you would need to map out how you will move forward to really selling lots of books. So as soon as you decide to write, you might learn a great deal about planning and staying focused.

There are indisputable benefits to writing. It is not likely as easy as it seems. There can be a handful of restrictions that you may possibly have to get around, like the investment of time required to train. You ought to allow yourself 2 days, and make a thorough commitment. Do not look to train sporadically. Devotion and sincere effort will eventually better position you to selling lots of books.

This will allow you some insight to determine if writing would be suitable for you. Unquestionably, writing requires an individual to be reader, content creator and expert. When you view yourself as the type of person with these specific qualities, you might be wholly ready to selling lots of books.

The most essential thing to be mindful of would be there are no shortcuts. Most people who have previously write understand how much devotion is essential. You ought to hear your innate voice, which would lead you through the preparations to writing.

Benefits of Writing

Every time you publish a book, there are generally some essential steps that you have to accomplish. You would need to talk to people who would want to read your book, brainstorm your book idea, and research other books in the market. These three steps don't only help folks out with writing, they alternatively bring other additional benefits to life. Publishing a book would be something which has made countless people near and far feel better about themselves.

Those who had been talk ingto people who would want to read your book may recognize slight changes in their mental well-being. These individuals alternatively feel equipped to tackle other things in life. Briefing ahead of time allows you to get stronger versus what you were before. It allows you to take on more than you were able to before, and not lose energy as easily. It all benefits you, and it alternatively helps you in your everyday activities.

You have previously identified yourself as a reader and content creator type of person. Any expert individual is typically geared to write.

People brainstorm your book idea when they train to write. Clearly, brainstorming your book idea has numerous benefits aside from solely getting organized and making sure you are presenting your best content. You will also find that you could show the benefits of the book. All this will make you become better on a regular basis.

Publishing a book alternatively results in getting topic ideas. It results from researching other books in the market, especially when done over a longer term of time. Also, it includes tons of other benefits. For starters, you will see what is selling well. Also you will get ideas for the book cover.

Writing would be an activity where anybody could constantly improve themselves through the preparatory process. Even though preparing can take up to 2 days, it means that you may probably have to train constantly for a term of time. Writing will make you be stronger and better equipped for your everyday challenges.

After Writing - What To Do

Writing is no simple task, and many times folks do not think about what exactly they would like to do after they selling lots of books. So much time is invested on preparing, yet hardly any thought is given to the recovery strategy. Even though focusing on publishing a book is essential, you should probably also think about what exactly you would like to experience afterwards. There would be no doubt you would feel better about yourself upon achieving your ambition to selling lots of books.

Be sure to facilitate time to recover from writing. If you are just starting at writing, then it would be best to take it slow. To decrease the time it may take to get back on track, here are some ideas to help you recover.

After writing, be sure to tell people about it!. You ought to also be sure to carry a copy with you wherever you go. It would physically help you recover much of the energy that you put forth on writing. In addition, be extremely careful not to don't get the book created, and not edit it. it does you no good in a drawer!. That will impede your whole recovery. Also, be sure you do not don't neglect to let people know you wrote a book- shout it from the rooftops!.

After writing, you might get burned out physically and intellectually. After spending 2 days preparing for your main objective, it is normal to want a little rest. When you are in your period of rest, it would be a beneficial idea to contemplate what exactly you may possibly want to accomplish next. Even though you do not have another specific aspiration in mind, it would be a beneficial idea to develop a sketchy idea where you wish to go next. Though remember, do not get into something new instantaneously. Make sure you are wholly recovered so you may make certain that you are actually ready. You could potentially cause harm to yourself through pushing too much. This would be the reason that moment of recreation is so essential.

That would be a benefit of permitting yourself to recharge. Then develop your plan. It can get hard to keep preparing without a clear-cut aspiration in mind. Once you craft a solid plan, you could get started right away.

You do not have to get immediately back to preparing as soon as you achieve your ambition. Spend a few hours to recover. Just remember not to strain yourself so you have the momentum to successfully accomplish your other goals!

Common Questions About Writing

At this point, you might be familiar with the preparations you ought to take to write. If you have a question which hasn't been covered, do not agonize. Here are a few typical questions which surface with writing:

Is it possible to write for free?

Commonly, it would be possible to write for free. It would be pointless to put in loads of cash preparing to write. Following are a couple instructions to manage expenses.

- Design your own book cover using Canva.

- Edit the book yourself.

- Self publish on Createspace.

Another question which typically comes up when people are getting ready to write is concerning the typical "rules" to recognize while publishing a book. Below are a handful of guidelines to bear in mind:

- While talk ingto people who would want to read your book, Listen intently to what they say. This would know the book will meet their needs.

- Typically, brainstorming your book idea would be essential when publishing a book. This would move forward confiedently.

- As you focus on researching other books in the market, be sure to Don't get discouraged if there are a lot of books like yours. This would know there is always room for your unique content.

You have begun the initial step toward writing by reading more on it. Probably more questions will surface and a different way you could help yourself would be by approaching this goal with a companion that may have similar objectives.

At times the "buddy system" would be a great solution while approaching a goal which requires a reader and content creator nature. Even though you will ultimately write on your own, it is beneficial to join someone on a parallel journey to go over questions as they pop up. Be conscious to pick like-minded friends and steer clear from individuals who are boring or non-reader, because such people might guide you away tackling your goals.

Remember all the questions you answered just a while ago?

Do you like to read books?

Do you have lots of content you want to share?

Do you need to establish yourself as an expert?

So you have replied yes to the questions which determined you had the most effective spirit to thrive at writing. Choose a companion that may also answer yes to these specific questions because such people may also be inclined to thrive at writing.

Congratulations on writing!

www.ingramcontent.com/pod-product-compliance
Lightning Source LLC
Chambersburg PA
CBHW070120210526
45170CB00013B/827